QUICKIE QUIZZES
FROM THE BIBLE #2

QUICKIE QUIZZES
FROM THE BIBLE #2

Compiled by
Charles Vander Meer

BAKER BOOK HOUSE
Grand Rapids, Michigan

ISBN: 0-8010-9266-3

Printed in the United States of America

CONTENTS

PREFACE

Questions, questions, questions. Children are full of them, but they also enjoy answering questions. This book gives them the opportunity to do just that.

The publication of this quiz book is accompanied by the prayer that each quiz will stimulate interest in God's Word, especially among boys and girls. The Bible is our tried and proven source of spiritual instruction. Because of the de-emphasis of God's Word in our public schools and in the media which increasingly influences our lives, we must use all of the means which the Lord provides us to learn about His Word.

These quizzes can be read by individuals or used in group situations such as the classroom, opening exercises of the Sunday school, or neighborhood Bible Clubs.

Some of the questions are more difficult than others. In quizzing young children, it may be well to eliminate some of the harder questions.

Happy quizzing!

Quizmaster "Uncle Charlie"

1 / THE BOOKS OF THE BIBLE

1. What book comes before Obadiah?

2. What book comes between Acts and I Corinthians?

3. What book comes after Esther?

4. The Book of Ephesians is between what two books?

5. What is the fortieth book of the Bible?

6. What book follows The Song of Solomon?

7. What book comes between Micah and Habakkuk?

8. What is the fifth book of the Bible?

9. What is the fifth book of the New Testament?

10. What books come before and after Ruth?

11. What is the thirty-eighth book of the Bible?

12. What book comes before Philemon?

13. What is the sixty-fifth book of the Bible?

14. What book comes between Jeremiah and Ezekiel?

15. What book follows II Peter?

16. What books come before and after Zephaniah?

2 / IN WHAT BOOK
DO YOU FIND . . .

1. the ten plagues?
2. a lion's den?
3. a pitcher, a trumpet, and 300 men?
4. the hymn book of the Israelites?
5. a dreamer, a pit, and a wonderful success story?
6. a wonderful love story involving a man named Boaz?
7. a boy, a giant, and five smooth stones?
8. the wisdom of a great king?
9. the walls of Jericho falling down?
10. a prophet telling of God crying over the sins of His people?
11. a picture of events to come?
12. the faith chapter?
13. a wheel within a wheel, and a valley of dry bones?
14. the prediction of where the Messiah would be born?
15. the words: "Vanity of vanities . . . all is vanity"?
16. a man hanged on the gallows he had built for another?
17. a man concerned about rebuilding the wall of Jerusalem?

3 / WHO AM I?

1. I am a goddess whom the Ephesians worshiped.

2. I was the only woman judge of the children of Israel.

3. I married Ruth, and we had a son named Obed, the grandfather of King David.

4. I returned to my people and to my gods, but Ruth would not leave Naomi.

5. My family and I were saved when Jericho was taken because I put a scarlet cord in the window.

6. I said to Paul, "Almost thou persuadest me to be a Christian."

7. My first child died, but later David and I had a son named Solomon.

8. I dreamed of a ladder reaching to heaven with angels ascending and descending.

9. My father sacrificed a ram in my place.

10. My sister's name was Mary, and my brother was Lazarus.

11. I helped a people escape captivity by leading them through both a sea and a desert.

12. Early in my life, I lost a rib so that I might have some company.

13. I was the one who placed Moses in an ark of bulrushes on the river bank.

14. I led the people in a march around the city of Jericho.

15. I was stoned to death because of my preaching.

16. I was a Pharisee, but realized I had a great spiritual need, and so I came to see Jesus at night.

4 / WHO LIVED FIRST?

1. Samuel or Solomon?
2. David or Daniel?
3. Jacob or Joshua?
4. Aaron or Abraham?
5. Hannah or Hagar?
6. Elijah or Elisha?
7. Joseph or Jonah?
8. Rachel or Rebekah?
9. Methuselah or Moses?
10. Ruth or Rahab?
11. Isaac or Isaiah?
12. Lot or Lazarus?
13. Shem or Seth?
14. Ham or Hophni?
15. Anna or Achan?
16. Melchizedek or Malchus?
17. Manoah or Mark?

5 / WHAT'S THE RELATIONSHIP
BETWEEN . . .

1. Aaron and Miriam?

2. James and John?

3. Noah and Shem?

4. Abraham and Lot?

5. Mary and Elisabeth?

6. Timothy and Lois?

7. Eli and Samuel?

8. Mary and Martha?

9. Jacob and Rachel?

10. Ruth and Naomi?

11. David and Jonathan?

12. Laban and Jacob?

13. Ananias and Sapphira?

14. Ham and Japheth?

15. Rebekah and Esau?

16. Andrew and Peter?

17. Methuselah and Noah?

6 / MOTHERS
IN THE BIBLE

Identify mothers in the Bible from these clues.

1. The mother of Moses, who hid him from the Egyptians for three months. (Exod. 6:20)

2. The mother of Samuel, the boy who helped Eli in the temple. (I Sam. 1:20)

3. The mother of Obed, and the great-grandmother of David. (Ruth 4:13-22)

4. The mother of John the Baptist, and the cousin of the mother of Jesus. (Luke 1:36)

5. The mother of Timothy (Paul's "son in the faith"). (II Tim. 1:5)

6. The mother of Seth. (Gen. 4:25)

7. The mother of Isaac, who laughed when she was told she would have a son in her old age. (Gen. 17:21)

8. The mother of Ishmael, whom Abram took to be his wife. (Gen. 16:8-11)

9. The mother of twins, Jacob and Esau. (Gen. 25:24)

10. The mother of Joseph and Benjamin. (Gen. 30:24; 35:18)

11. The mother of Jacob's first son. (Gen. 29:32)

12. The mother of the wisest man who ever lived. (II Sam. 12:24)

13. The wife of Joseph, and mother of Manasseh and Ephraim. (Gen. 41:50-52)

14. The mother of Mahlon and Chilion, brothers who were married to Ruth and Orpah. (Ruth 1:2)

15. The mother of the Lord Jesus. (Matt. 1:18)

7 / BIBLE DETECTIVE

Identify Bible characters from these clues.

1. A shipwreck at Melita.
2. Pillars; blindness.
3. Mount Sinai; the Ten Commandments.
4. Little; a sycamore tree.
5. A prophet; Lamentations.
6. A physician; the Book of Acts.
7. A kiss; pieces of silver.
8. The isle of Patmos; Revelation.
9. A twin; hairy.
10. Locusts and wild honey; the command "Repent!"
11. Handwriting; a feast.
12. Pairs; a promise.
13. Martyr; stoning.
14. A great fish; Nineveh.
15. A pit; Egypt.
16. Two spies; Jericho.
17. Gleaning; Naomi.
18. A voice in the night; the words "Speak Lord."

8 / WHO AM I?

1. Jesus saw me coming, and said of me, "Behold an Israelite indeed, in whom is no guile."

2. I told the chief priests and the people that I found no fault in Jesus.

3. Jacob served my father for seven years, and received Leah as his wife; then he served seven more years, and I became his wife.

4. I was the mother of twin sons, Jacob and Esau.

5. I was the first son of Jacob and Leah.

6. I made a feast and promised to give thirty sheets and thirty changes of garment to the one who could answer my riddle.

7. I was the son of David and Bathsheba.

8. Paul and I prayed and sang praises to God at midnight.

9. I am the apostle to whom Jesus said, "I am the way, the truth and the life."

10. Once my husband and I worried that our son had been lost as we were returning from Jerusalem.

11. Once I took a missionary journey with Paul and Barnabas, until these two quarreled about me; then I went with Barnabas.

12. After seeing my city destroyed by fire and brimstone, I went to live in a mountain with my two daughters.

13. I became a great ruler in Egypt because I was able to interpret dreams.

14. I have often been referred to as the "beloved physician," and I traveled with Paul on some of his missionary journeys.

15. God promised me that my descendants would be more in number than the dust of the earth.

16. I went to war with only three hundred men, armed with pitchers, torches, and trumpets.

9 / HOW MANY . . .

1. days was Jesus tempted in the wilderness? (Mark 1:13)

2. windows were built into the ark? (Gen. 6:16)

3. years did Noah live after the flood? (Gen. 9:28)

4. days did God take to create everything? (Exod. 20:11)

5. pillars did Samson pull down in the temple of Dagon? (Judg. 16:29)

6. Philistines did Samson slay with the jawbone of an ass? (Judg. 15:15)

7. chapters are found in the Book of Psalms?

8. men came to comfort and advise Job?

9. descendants did God promise Abram? (Gen. 13:16; 15:5)

10. people were in the ark? (Gen. 7:7)

11. chapters are found in the Book of Obadiah?

12. men did the king see in the fiery furnace? (Dan. 3:25)

13. plagues did God send upon the Egyptians?

14. daughters did Jacob have? (Gen. 30:20-21)

15. waterpots did Jesus command the servants to fill with water at the wedding in Cana? (John 2:6-7)

16. days of the week were the Israelites to gather manna? (Exod. 16:26)

17. baskets did the Egyptian baker see in his dream? (Gen. 40:16)

10 / TO WHOM
DID GOD SAY . . .

1. "But of the tree of the knowledge of good and evil, thou shalt not eat of it: for in the day thou eatest thereof thou shalt surely die." (Gen. 2:17)

2. "Where is Abel thy brother?" (Gen. 4:9)

3. "I do set my bow in the cloud, and it shall be for a token of a covenant between me and the earth." (Gen. 9:13)

4. "Take now thy son, thine only son . . . whom thou lovest, and get thee into the land of Moriah; and offer him there for a burnt offering upon one of the mountains which I will tell thee of." (Gen. 22:2)

5. "Arise, go up to Bethel, and dwell there: and make there an altar unto God, that appeared unto thee when thou fleddest from the face of Esau thy brother." (Gen. 35:1)

6. "Draw not nigh hither: put off thy shoes from off thy feet, for the place whereon thou standest is holy ground." (Exod. 3:5)

7. ". . . As I was with Moses, so I will be with thee: I will not fail thee, nor forsake thee." (Josh. 1:5)

8. "Go in this thy might, and thou shalt save Israel from the hand of the Midianites: have not I sent thee?" (Judg. 6:14)

9. "Behold, I will do a thing in Israel, at which both the ears of every one that heareth it shall tingle. In that day I will perform against Eli all things which I have spoken concerning his house. . . ." (I Sam. 3:11-12)

10. "Because thou hast asked this thing, and hast not asked for thyself long life; neither hast asked riches for thyself, nor hast asked the life of thine enemies; but has asked for thyself understanding to discern judgment. . . ." (I Kings 3:11)

11. "Hast thou considered my servant Job, that there is none like him in the earth, a perfect and an upright man, one that feareth God? . . ." (Job. 1:8)

12. ". . . Thou shalt not build me an house to dwell in: For I have not dwelt in an house since the day that I brought up Israel unto this day; but have gone from tent to tent, and from one tabernacle to another." (I Chron. 17:4-5)

11 / WHO AM I?

1. I stole a garment and some gold and hid them in my tent, but the Lord knew about it.

2. I tricked my nephew Jacob into marrying both of my daughters.

3. I wrote the last book of the minor prophets.

4. I lived longer than any other person.

5. Because I was so unhappy, I wanted to change my name to Mara, which means *bitter.*

6. While Peter preached mainly to Jews, I felt especially called to be a missionary to the Gentiles.

7. Jesus healed my mother-in-law when she was sick with a fever.

8. My father's name was Laban, and my sister was Leah.

9. I lived on the wall of Jericho and helped hide the men who came to spy in our land.

10. I kept my younger brothers from killing our brother, Joseph, by suggesting they cast him into a pit.

11. When I was still quite young, my mother took me to the temple to help the priest, Eli.

12. I once visited a witch instead of seeking help from the Lord.

13. I am known as the "doubting" disciple.

14. Paul called me his "son in the faith."

15. I was the first Christian martyr.

16. Paul wrote to my master, Philemon, and asked him to forgive me for running away.

17. I'm noted in Hebrews 11, the faith chapter, as one who offered a more excellent sacrifice to God than my brother.

12 / WHAT'S THE MISSING WORD?

1. "Am I my brother's _____ ?" (Gen. 4:9)

2. "I know that my Redeemer _____ ." (Job. 19:25)

3. "Redeeming the time, because the days are _____ ." (Eph. 5:16)

4. "A soft answer turneth away _____ ." (Prov. 15:1)

5. "For by grace are ye saved through _____ ." (Eph. 2:8)

6. "I will put enmity between thee and the _____ ." (Gen. 3:15)

7. "Blessed are they that mourn: for they shall be _____ ." (Matt. 5:4)

8. "Create in me a clean _____ , O God." (Ps. 51:10)

9. "Behold the Lamb of God, which taketh away the sin of the _____ ." (John 1:29)

10. "Choose you this day whom ye will _____ ." (Josh. 24:15)

11. "For unto us a child is born, unto us a son is _____ ." (Isa. 9:6)

12. "And now abideth faith, hope, charity, these three: but the greatest of these is _____ ." (I Cor. 13:13)

13. "In the beginning was the _____ ." (John 1:1)

14. "Behold, I stand at the door, and _____ ." (Rev. 3:20)

15. "Ye are the _____ of the earth." (Matt. 5:13)

16. "Though your sins be as scarlet, they shall be as white as _____ ." (Isa. 1:18)

13 / FINISH THE PHRASE!

1. "He is not here: for he is _____." (Matt. 28:6)

2. "THIS IS JESUS THE KING _____ _____ _____." (Matt. 27:37)

3. "He that winneth souls is _____." (Prov. 11:30)

4. "I am the way, the truth, and the _____." (John 14:6)

5. "Study to shew thyself approved unto God, a workman that needeth not to be _____." (II Tim. 2:15)

6. "I beseech you therefore, brethren, by the mercies of God, that ye present your bodies a living sacrifice, holy, acceptable unto God, which is your _____ _____." (Rom. 12:1)

7. "Before the cock crow, thou shalt deny me _____." (Matt. 26:75)

8. "He brought me up also out of an horrible pit, out of the miry _____." (Ps. 40:2)

9. "And he shall be like a tree planted by the _____ _____ _____." (Ps. 1:3)

10. Job's wife said to him, "Curse God, and _____." (Job. 2:9)

11. "As I was with Moses, so I will be with _____." (Josh. 1:5)

12. "Thy people shall be _____ _____." (Ruth 1:16)

13. "Bless the Lord, O my soul: and all that is within me, bless _____ _____ _____." (Ps. 103:1)

14. "For I am not ashamed of the _____ _____ _____." (Rom. 1:16)

15. "Be not deceived, God is not _____." (Gal. 6:7)

16. "Children, obey your parents in the Lord: for this _____ _____." (Eph. 6:1)

14 / WHO AM I?

1. I was known as my brother's "spokesman."

2. Along with Aaron, I helped to hold up Moses' arms so that the Israelites could win a battle.

3. I had a strange experience in which my donkey talked to me.

4. My father didn't want me to go back to Egypt with my brothers.

5. Along with my three Hebrew friends, Shadrach, Meshach, and Abednego, I would not eat the rich food offered by the king.

6. I failed to restrain my evil sons, even though I was high priest in the temple.

7. I was made queen in place of Vashti.

8. When God called me to be a judge of Israel, I asked Him for a special sign which involved a fleece of wool.

9. In an attempt to kill the baby Jesus, I had all little children two years of age and under put to death.

10. When told that I was about to die, I asked the Lord for more years to live, and He granted me fifteen additional years.

11. My father sent his servant back to our homeland to obtain a wife for me.

12. I once used a stone for a pillow.

13. I am known as the "weeping" prophet.

14. I was the father of the boy who slew a giant named Goliath.

15. I was afflicted with boils from the top of my head to the bottom of my feet.

16. I was very unhappy because my father, who was king, hated my best friend.

15 / PRAYERS
IN THE BIBLE

1. Who prayed that the wicked city of Sodom might not be destroyed? (Gen. 18:23-33)

2. Who prayed that God would help him find a bride for his master's son? (Gen. 24:1-14)

3. Who prayed that God would make the fleece of wool wet and the ground dry, as a sign that God would be with him in leading the Israelites? (Judg. 6:36-37)

4. Who prayed for a child so earnestly that the priest of the temple thought she was drunk? (I Sam. 1:13)

5. Who said in one of his prayers, "Create in me a clean heart, O God"? (Ps. 51:10)

6. Who prayed three times a day, in front of his window, facing Jerusalem? (Dan. 6:10)

7. Who prayed in the Garden of Gethsemane? (Luke 22:39-46)

8. Who prayed, "Lord, save me," when he began to sink into the water? (Matt. 14:28-30)

9. What was the name of the father of John the Baptist, who prayed that his wife might have a son? (Luke 1:13)

10. Who prayed from hell that someone warn his brothers so that they might not have to come to that place of torment? (Luke 16:22-31)

11. How many lepers prayed to Jesus for healing? (Luke 17:12-13)

12. Who was chosen to take the place of Judas, after the disciples asked God to direct their choice? (Acts 1:23-26)

13. Who prayed for his persecutors even while they were stoning him? (Acts 7:59-60)

14. Who prayed three times that the Lord would remove a "thorn in the flesh"? (II Cor. 12:7-8)

15. In what book of the Bible do we find the prayer, "Even so, come, Lord Jesus"? (Rev. 22:20)

16 / FACTS IN GENESIS

Creation

1. What name did God give to the firmament? (Gen. 1:8)

2. What name did God give to the dry land? (Gen. 1:10)

3. On what day of creation was man formed of the dust of the ground? (Gen. 1:26-31)

4. What are the first recorded words of God in Genesis 1? (Gen. 1:3)

5. What animal was called more "subtil" than any beast of the field? (Gen. 3:1)

6. On what day did God rest from his labors of creation? (Gen. 2:2)

7. Of what tree in the Garden of Eden were Adam and Eve not to eat? (Gen. 2:17)

8. What did Adam and Eve sew together to make aprons for themselves? (Gen. 3:7)

9. What did God use to clothe Adam and Eve? (Gen. 3:21)

The Flood

10. Why did God have to send a flood upon the earth? (Gen. 6:12-13)

11. What was the ark to be made of? (Gen. 6:14)

12. How many windows were to be built into the ark? (Gen. 6:16)

13. How old was Noah when the flood came? (Gen. 7:6)

14. What were the names of Noah's three sons? (Gen. 6:10)

15. How many persons went into the ark altogether? (Gen. 7:13)

16. What two birds did Noah send out from the ark? (Gen. 8:7-8)

17 / PEOPLE IN GENESIS

1. Who lived to the ripe old age of 930 years? (Gen. 5:5)

2. Who died at a comparatively young age, 364 years old? (Gen. 5:23)

3. Which son of Noah has a name that reminds us of something we like to eat? (Gen. 5:32)

4. Name two men who had their names changed by the Lord. (Gen. 17:5; 35:10)

5. Who was the lady whose name was changed by the Lord? (Gen. 17:15)

6. Who chose all the good, well-watered land for himself when his uncle offered him first choice? (Gen. 13:10-11)

7. Who cast her child under a shrub, thinking that God no longer cared about her? (Gen. 21:14-15)

8. Who was commanded by God to offer his son as a sacrifice? (Gen. 22:2)

9. What was the name of the woman Abraham took as his wife after Sarah died? (Gen. 25:1)

10. Whose bride was chosen for him by his father's servant? (Gen. 24:4)

11. Who sold his birthright for bread and pottage? (Gen. 25:34)

12. Who obtained his father's blessing by being deceitful? (Gen. 27:19)

13. What was the name of Jacob's uncle, who tricked him into marrying both of his daughters? (Gen. 29:16)

14. Which one of these daughters did Jacob really love most? (Gen. 29:18)

15. What was the name of the young fellow who dreamed strange dreams about his brothers bowing down to him? (Gen. 37:5-7)

16. What was the name of the brother of Joseph who was kept in Egypt while the others went back to Canaan to get Benjamin? (Gen. 42:24)

18 / FACTS IN EXODUS

1. When Moses and Aaron first went to see Pharaoh, how many days of travel did they ask him to allow the children of Israel? (Exod. 5:3)

2. Pharaoh's answer was to make the children of Israel work even harder. What were they forced to gather, in order to make bricks? (Exod. 5:7)

3. When Moses and Aaron went before Pharaoh again, he wanted to see them perform a miracle. Aaron cast his rod, or staff, upon the ground. What did it become? (Exod. 7:10)

4. What happened to the waters of the river during the first plague that God sent? (Exod. 7:20)

5. What came up out of the river during the second plague, and got into the people's houses, beds, and even into their ovens? (Exod. 8:2)

6. What was the ninth plague that God sent against Pharaoh and Egypt? (Exod. 10:21-22)

7. The tenth plague brought death to whom? (Exod. 12:29)

8. In order to be safe from the death angel who passed over, what did the children of Israel sprinkle on the sides and top of their doors? (Exod. 12:3-7)

9. At what hour did the death angel pass over? (Exod. 12:29)

10. What did the children of Israel bake for their departure from Egypt? (Exod. 12:39)

11. What happened to Pharaoh and the army as they ran after the Israelites? (Exod. 14:28)

12. What did Moses cast into the water at Marah to make it sweet? (Exod. 15:25)

13. What did the people call the bread which God sent to feed them? (Exod. 16:15)

14. What two things led the children of Israel as they traveled from Egypt to Canaan? (Exod. 13:21)

15. How long did the children of Israel eat manna in the wilderness? (Exod. 16:35)

19 / PEOPLE AND PLACES
IN EXODUS

1. What was the name given to the leader of the Egyptian people? (Exod. 1:11)

2. Who took his first boat ride in a basket made with reeds and tar? (Exod. 2:10)

3. What was the name of Moses' father-in-law? (Exod. 3:1)

4. Whom did the Lord appoint as "spokesman" for Moses? (Exod. 4:14-16)

5. Who was the sister of Moses and Aaron? (Exod. 15:20)

6. What was the name of the sea that Moses parted by stretching out his hands? (Exod. 15:22)

7. What was the name of the place where Moses changed the bitter waters to sweet? (Exod. 15:23)

8. Who helped hold up Moses' arms during one of the Israelites' battles? (Exod. 17:12)

9. On what mountain did Moses receive the Ten Commandments from God? (Exod. 31:18)

10. Who found Moses in a little reed basket? (Exod. 2:5)

11. The name of Moses' wife sounds like something a lady would sew onto a skirt or pants. What is her name? (Exod. 2:21)

12. From what tribe was Moses' family descended? (Exod. 2:1)

13. Who tried to copy the miracles of Moses and Aaron when they went before Pharaoh? (Exod. 7:11)

14. Whose bones did Moses take with him out of Egypt? (Exod. 13:19)

15. What was the name of the portion of Egypt where the Israelites lived? (Exod. 8:22)

20 / WHO SAID IT?

1. "This is now bone of my bones, and flesh of my flesh. . . ." (Gen. 2:23)

2. "My punishment is greater than I can bear." (Gen. 4:13)

3. "Say, I pray thee, thou art my sister: that it may be well with me for thy sake. . . ." (Gen. 12:13)

4. "Up, get you out of this place; for the Lord will destroy this city." (Gen. 19:14)

5. "Behold the fire and the wood: but where is the lamb for a burnt offering?" (Gen. 22:7)

6. "I will draw water for thy camels also, until they have done drinking." (Gen. 24:19)

7. "Sell me this day thy birthright." (Gen. 25:31)

8. ". . . He took away my birthright; and, behold, now he hath taken away my blessing." (Gen. 27:36)

9. "Behold, I have dreamed a dream more; and, behold, the sun and the moon and the eleven stars made obeisance to me." (Gen. 37:9)

10. "I also was in my dream, and, behold, I had three white baskets on my head." (Gen. 40:16)

11. "Shall I go and call to thee a nurse of the Hebrew women, that she may nurse the child for thee?" (Exod. 2:7)

12. "Take this child away, and nurse it for me, and I will give thee thy wages." (Exod. 2:9)

13. "I will now turn aside, and see this great sight, why the bush is not burnt." (Exod. 3:3)

14. "Who is the Lord, that I should obey his voice to let Israel go? . . ." (Exod. 5:2)

15. "These be thy gods, O Israel, which brought thee up out of the land of Egypt." (Exod. 32:4)

21 / MEN AND WOMEN
OF ISRAEL

1. Joshua, the man who followed Moses, was the son of a man with a strange name. What was it? (Josh. 1:1)

2. The two spies that Joshua sent out stayed in the home of a woman whose house was on the wall of the city of Jericho. What was her name? (Josh. 2:1)

3. One man disobeyed Joshua's command about not taking any gold from the city of Jericho. He took some, and hid it in his tent. What was his name? (Josh. 7:20)

4. Joshua and another man were the only spies who believed that the Israelites could conquer the land of Canaan. Later, Joshua gave this man the land of Hebron as an inheritance. What was his name? (Josh. 14:13)

5. What was the name of the first judge, or deliverer, whom God sent to help the children of Israel? (Judg. 3:9)

6. The king of Moab, one of the enemies of the Israelites, was described as "a very fat man." What was his name. (Judg. 3:17)

7. When Barak would not go alone into battle for the Israelites, God sent a woman along with him. This woman was the first woman judge. What was her name? (Judg. 4:9)

8. What great judge did God send to help the Israelites overcome the Midianites? (Judg. 6:34)

9. One of Israel's judges made a foolish promise to the Lord, promising to sacrifice the first thing that came to meet him after battle. What was this judge's name? (Judg. 11:30)

10. One of the most famous of Israel's judges killed many of the enemy with the jawbone of an animal. What was his name? (Judg. 15:16)

11. One of Israel's judges was tricked by a woman who found out the secret of his strength. Who was she? (Judg. 16:4)

22 / DAVID, THE MAN
AFTER GOD'S OWN HEART

1. What was the name of David's father? (I Sam. 16:19)

2. What was the name of the first king of Israel, who became one of David's greatest enemies? (I Sam. 11:15)

3. What was the name of the king's son, a good friend of David? (I Sam. 19:2)

4. Whom did David defeat with a stone and a sling? (I Sam. 17:4)

5. How many stones did David put in his pouch? (I Sam. 17:40)

6. What book of the Bible did David help to write?

7. What was the name of the enemy nation against whom David fought often during his lifetime? (I Sam. 19:8)

8. What musical instrument did David play quite well? (I Sam. 16:23)

9. What great prophet anointed David king of Israel? (I Sam. 16:13)

10. David sinned by wanting to marry a woman who was already married. What was her name? (II Sam. 11:3)

11. What was the name of this woman's husband, whom David placed at the front of the battle so that he would be killed? (II Sam. 11:3)

12. What was the name of the prophet who said to David, "Thou art the man"? (II Sam. 12:7)

13. What was the name of the son of David who hanged in a tree by his long hair? (II Sam. 18:33)

14. What was the name of the son of David who became a very wise king? (I Kings 2:12)

15. Who will someday sit upon the throne of King David? (Luke 1:31-32)

23 / ELIJAH AND ELISHA

1. What kind of bird fed Elijah during a period of famine and drought? (I Kings 17:4)

2. After being fed by a bird, Elijah was cared for by the widow of Zarephath. What miracle did Elijah perform so that she and her son would not starve? (I Kings 17:16)

3. What wicked king hated Elijah, and accepted the challenge to a contest between his prophets of Baal and Elijah? (I Kings 18:20)

4. How many prophets of Baal were contending against Elijah? (I Kings 18:19)

5. What was the name of the mountain where the contest between Elijah and the prophets of Baal took place? (I Kings 18:19)

6. When Baal didn't answer the prophets, what did Elijah say their god was doing? (I Kings 18:27)

7. What was the name of Ahab's wife, the wicked queen who also hated Elijah? (I Kings 19:1)

8. How was Elijah taken to heaven? (II Kings 2:11)

9. What article of Elijah's clothing was given to Elisha as a sign that he too would have power from God? (II Kings 2:13)

10. What was the name of the captain of the Syrian army, whom God healed of leprosy through His agent, Elisha? (II Kings 5:1)

11. How many times did Elisha tell this captain to wash in the river? (II Kings 5:10)

12. What was the name of the river? (II Kings 5:10)

13. What was the name of Elisha's servant, who lied to Naaman and, as a result, became a leper himself? (II Kings 5:20)

14. Some children made fun of Elisha's baldness. What happened to them? (II Kings 2:24)

15. What miracle did Elisha perform when an axe head fell into the water? (II Kings 6:6)

24 / DANIEL AND JONAH

1. Who conspired against Daniel because he was so popular with the king? (Dan. 6:4)

2. What was the name of this king? (Dan. 6:6)

3. What was the first thing Daniel did when he heard about the decree the king had signed, making it illegal for Daniel to pray to his God? (Dan. 6:10)

4. Was King Darius happy or sad when he learned that Daniel would have to be thrown into the lion's den? (Dan. 6:14)

5. What did God send to shut the lions' mouths? (Dan. 6:22)

6. Who were thrown to the lions in Daniel's place? (Dan. 6:24)

7. To what city did God command Jonah to go? (Jonah 1:2)

8. Where did Jonah decide to go instead? (Jonah 1:3)

9. At what seaport did Jonah board a ship? (Jonah 1:3)

10. What was Jonah doing when the storm first struck the ship? (Jonah 1:5)

11. What did Jonah suggest the mariners do to him to calm the storm? (Jonah 1:12)

12. What was the first thing Jonah did while in the belly of the whale? (Jonah 2:1)

13. How long was Jonah in the belly of the whale? (Jonah 1:17)

14. What did Jonah do the second time God told him to go to Nineveh? (Jonah 3:3)

15. What did the people of Nineveh do when Jonah preached to them? (Jonah 3:10)

25 / THE BOY JESUS

1. Who was the mother of Jesus? (Matt. 1:18)

2. Who was Mary's husband? (Matt. 1:19)

3. What name, given to Jesus at his birth, means "God with us"? (Matt. 1:23)

4. Who gave the decree that all were to be taxed? (Luke 2:1)

5. What city is known as the "city of David"? (Luke 2:4)

6. What were the first two words the angel spoke to the shepherds? (Luke 2:10)

7. Where did the shepherds find the baby Jesus lying? (Luke 2:12)

8. Where did Mary and Joseph take Jesus to escape the anger of Herod? (Matt. 2:14)

9. What gifts did the wise men bring to the child Jesus? (Matt. 2:11)

10. In what city did Jesus grow up? (Luke 2:39)

11. Where did Jesus' parents travel every year? (Luke 2:41)

12. What took place there every year? (Luke 2:41)

13. How old was Jesus when his parents took him with them? (Luke 2:42)

14. How long had Jesus' parents been journeying home before they realized that he was not with them? (Luke 2:44)

15. How many days passed before they found Him? (Luke 2:46)

16. What had He been doing? (Luke 2:46)

17. Finish this verse: "And Jesus increased in wisdom and stature, and in favour with ___ ___ ___ ." (Luke 2:52)

26 / HIS PARABLES

1. On what kind of foundation did the wise man build his house? (Matt. 7:24)

2. On what kind of foundation did the foolish man build? (Matt. 7:26)

3. What happened to the seed which fell by the wayside in the parable of the sower? (Luke 8:5)

4. In the parable of the sower, what did the seed stand for? (Luke 8:11)

5. The good ground refers to what kind of people in this parable? (Luke 8:14)

6. In the parable of the rich man, what did this man decide to do? (Luke 12:18)

7. In the parable of the lost sheep, where were the ninety-nine sheep left? (Luke 15:4)

8. Name two things the woman did before she found the lost coin. (Luke 15:8)

9. What work was the prodigal son doing after he had spent all his money? (Luke 15:15)

10. In the parable of the Pharisee and the publican, which one was proud? (Luke 18:11)

11. In the parable of the two sons, in which the father told his sons to work in his vineyard, one son said he wouldn't go but he did. How did the other son respond? (Matt. 21:30)

12. Our testimony for Christ should not be "hid under a bushel," but put "on a candlestick" instead. What does this mean? (Matt. 5:15-16)

13. True or false? In the parable of the marriage of the king's son, those who were first invited to the feast were very happy to come. (Matt. 22:3)

14. One of the guests who did come to the wedding feast was lacking something. What was it? (Matt. 22:11)

27 / THE MIRACLE-WORKER

1. What means did the friends of the man sick with palsy use to place him before Jesus? (Luke 5:19)

2. What did Jesus tell the deformed man to do with his withered hand? (Luke 6:10)

3. What did the Lord do for the son of the widow of Nain? (Luke 7:14-15)

4. Into what animals did Jesus send the demons after casting them out of the two men? (Matt. 8:32)

5. What part of Jesus' garment had the healed woman touched? (Luke 8:43-44)

6. About how old was Jairus' daughter, whom Jesus healed? (Luke 8:42)

7. How did the people react when Jesus told them the girl was only sleeping? (Luke 8:53)

8. In the feeding of the 5,000, how many loaves and how many fishes were there? (Luke 9:13)

9. In the miracle of the ten lepers whom Jesus healed, what nationality was the man who came back to thank the Lord? (Luke 17:16)

10. In the healing of the blind begger, what did he keep crying out to Jesus? (Luke 18:38)

11. What was Jesus doing before He calmed the storm? (Matt. 8:24)

12. What did Peter do when he saw Jesus coming toward the ship, walking on the water? (Matt. 14:29)

13. How many loaves were there at the feeding of the 4,000? (Matt. 15:36)

14. During the wedding at Cana of Galilee, what did Jesus tell the servants to do with the waterpots? (John 2:7)

15. What order did Jesus give to the man who had been waiting to be healed for thirty-eight years? (John 5:8)

16. In what pool did Jesus tell the blind man to wash his eyes? (John 9:11)

17. How long had Lazarus been dead when Jesus raised him? (John 11:39)

28 / JESUS OUR LORD

1. Who were the two groups who took counsel against Jesus to put Him to death? (Matt. 27:1)

2. What was the name of the Roman governor, who later washed his hands and said he wanted nothing to do with putting Jesus to death? (Matt. 27:2)

3. What was the name of the disciple who betrayed Jesus to His enemies? (Matt. 27:3)

4. For how many pieces of silver did he betray Jesus? (Matt. 27:3)

5. After he realized the wrong thing he had done, what did this disciple do? (Matt. 27:5)

6. What is the name of the prisoner whom the governor released in place of Jesus? (Matt. 27:26)

7. How many thieves were crucified with Jesus? (Matt. 27:38)

8. While the Lord was on the cross, for how many hours was it dark? (Matt. 27:45)

9. Just before He died, Jesus spoke these words: "Eli, Eli, lama sabachthani." What does this mean? (Matt. 27:46)

10. Who took the body of Jesus and laid it in his own tomb? (Matt. 27:57-60)

11. On what day of the week was Jesus raised from the dead? (Matt. 28:1)

12. Who had rolled back the huge stone from the door of the tomb? (Matt. 28:2)

13. With whom did the angel tell the women to share the news that Christ had risen? (Matt. 28:7)

14. What was the lie which the chief counsel paid the guards to tell about Jesus? (Matt. 28:13)

15. After His resurrection, Jesus appeared to His disciples, but one of them doubted Jesus' resurrection and was not there. Who was this? (John 20:24)

16. After His resurrection, to whom did Jesus say, "Feed my sheep"? (John 21:16)

29 / WHO SAID IT?

1. "Behold the handmaid of the Lord; be it unto me according to thy word." (Luke 1:38)

2. "Blessed art thou among women, and blessed is the fruit of thy womb." (Luke 1:41-42)

3. "Behold the Lamb of God, which taketh away the sin of the world." (John 1:29)

4. "Rabbi, we know that thou art a teacher come from God: for no man can do these miracles that thou doest, except God be with him." (John 3:1-2)

5. "Thou art the Christ, the Son of the living God." (Matt. 16:16)

6. "What will ye give me, and I will deliver him unto you?" (Matt. 26:14-15)

7. "What shall I do then with Jesus which is called Christ?" (Matt. 27:22)

8. "He is not here, for He is risen. . . ." (Matt. 28:5-6)

9. "Master, it is good for us to be here: and let us make three tabernacles; one for thee, and one for Moses, and one for Elias." (Mark 9:5)

10. "Jesus, thou son of David, have mercy on me." (Mark 10:46-47)

11. "Let us now go even unto Bethlehem, and see this thing which is come to pass. . . ." (Luke 2:15)

12. "Take care of him; and whatsoever thou spendest more, when I come again, I will repay thee." (Luke 10:33-35)

13. "God be merciful to me a sinner." (Luke 18:13)

14. "Behold, Lord, the half of my goods I give to the poor. . . ." (Luke 19:8)

15. "Heaven and earth shall pass away; but my words shall not pass away." (Luke 21:29-33)

30 / FACTS ABOUT
THE EARLY CHURCH

1. Between which two books of the Bible do you find the Book of Acts?

2. Was this book written before or after Jesus went back to heaven?

3. Where did Jesus tell the disciples to wait until the Holy Spirit came? (Acts 1:1-4)

4. One of the first items of business that Peter and the disciples had to handle was the replacement of Judas. Whom did the disciples choose to take Judas' place? (Acts 1:26)

5. What very unique gift did the disciples receive on the day of Pentecost, when the Holy Spirit came in fulfillment of the promise Jesus had made? (Acts 2:4)

6. As Jesus was being taken up into heaven, what did the angels promise the disciples? (Acts 1:11)

7. About how many people were added to the church after Peter preached his first message? (Acts 2:41)

8. What did Peter and John do for the lame man who begged an offering from them? (Acts 3:7)

9. What happened to Ananias and Sapphira when they lied to the disciples? (Acts 5:5, 10)

10. Stephen was not afraid to stand up for what he believed. Because of this stand, he was put to death. How was Stephen put to death? (Acts 7:59)

11. While they were killing Stephen, the people laid their garments at the feet of a man who was later to become the first Christian missionary. Who was this? (Acts 7:58)

12. Who was involved in a great revival in Samaria, but was called by God to witness to one individual? (Acts 8:25-26)

13. Which book of the Bible was the Ethiopian eunuch reading when Philip approached him? (Acts 8:27-28)

31 / FACTS ABOUT PAUL
THE MISSIONARY

1. Where was Saul (Paul) headed and what was he planning to do when the Lord caused a bright light to shine upon him? (Acts 9:1-3)

2. For how long was Paul blind after the Lord appeared to him? (Acts 9:9)

3. What was the name of the lady living in Joppa, whom Peter raised from the dead? (Acts 9:36-40)

4. In the vision that Peter experienced while on the housetop, the Lord told him to "rise, and eat." What was Peter's reply? (Acts 10:14)

5. What was the name of the city where the disciples were first called *Christians?* (Acts 11:26)

6. What did the people say to Rhoda when she explained that Peter was knocking at the door of the room which they were using to pray for Peter's release? (Acts 12:15)

7. Who were the first two men sent out as missionaries by the Christian church? (Acts 13:2)

8. At what hour of the night did Paul and Silas pray and sing praises while imprisoned during Paul's second missionary journey? (Acts 16:25)

9. What occurred while they were singing and praying? (Acts 16:26)

10. What was the jailor about to do, thinking that all of the prisoners had fled? (Acts 16:27)

11. What was his first question to Paul and Silas? (Acts 16:30)

12. What was their reply? (Acts 16:31)

13. Where did Paul see an altar with the inscription, "TO THE UN-KNOWN GOD"? (Acts 17:22-23)

14. What was the name of the goddess worshiped by the Ephesians? (Acts 19:26-27)

15. Who was the king who responded to Paul's preaching by saying, "Almost thou persuadest me to be a Christian"? (Acts 26:28)

16. On his way to Rome, Paul was shipwrecked on the island of Melita. While gathering sticks for a fire, something happened that should have ended his life, but didn't. What was it? (Acts 28:1-5)

32 / WHO SAID IT?*

1. "But ye shall receive power, after that the Holy Ghost is come upon you. . . ." (Acts 1:1-8)

2. "Ye men of Judaea, and all ye that dwell at Jerusalem, be this known unto you, and hearken to my words." (Acts 2:14)

3. ". . . If this counsel or this work be of men, it will come to nought: but if it be of God, ye cannot overthrow it. . . ." (Acts 5:34-39)

4. "Lord, lay not this sin to their charge." (Acts 7:59-60)

5. "Understandest thou what thou readest?" (Acts 8:30)

6. "How can I, except some man should guide me?" (Acts 8:31)

7. "Who art thou, Lord?" (Acts 9:5)

8. "Sirs, what must I do to be saved?" (Acts 16:27-30)

9. "If it were a matter of wrong or wicked lewdness, O ye Jews, reason would that I should bear with you. . . ." (Acts 18:14)

10. "Sirs, ye know that by this craft we have our wealth. Moreover ye see and hear, that not alone at Ephesus, but almost throughout all Asia, this Paul hath persuaded and turned away much people. . . ." (Acts 19:24-26)

11. "Go thy way for this time; when I have a convenient season, I will call for thee." (Acts 24:25)

12. "Paul, thou art beside thyself; much learning doth make thee mad." (Acts 26:24)

13. "Almost thou persuadest me to be a Christian." (Acts 26:28)

*This quiz is for more advanced Bible students.

ANSWERS

1. **THE BOOKS OF THE BIBLE**
   1. Amos
   2. Romans
   3. Job
   4. Galatians and Philippians
   5. Matthew
   6. Isaiah
   7. Nahum
   8. Deuteronomy
   9. Acts
   10. Judges; I Samuel
   11. Zechariah
   12. Titus
   13. Jude
   14. Lamentations
   15. I John
   16. Habakkuk; Haggai

2. **IN WHAT BOOK ...?**
   1. Exodus
   2. Daniel
   3. Judges
   4. Psalms
   5. Genesis
   6. Ruth
   7. I Samuel
   8. Proverbs (or Ecclesiastes)
   9. Joshua
   10. Jeremiah
   11. Revelation
   12. Hebrews
   13. Ezekiel
   14. Micah
   15. Ecclesiastes
   16. Esther
   17. Nehemiah

3. **WHO AM I?**
   1. Diana
   2. Deborah
   3. Boaz
   4. Orpah
   5. Rahab
   6. Agrippa
   7. Bathsheba
   8. Jacob
   9. Isaac
   10. Martha
   11. Moses
   12. Adam
   13. Miriam
   14. Joshua
   15. Stephen
   16. Nicodemus

4. **WHO LIVED FIRST?**
   1. Samuel
   2. David
   3. Jacob
   4. Abraham
   5. Hagar
   6. Elijah
   7. Joseph
   8. Rebekah
   9. Methuselah
   10. Rahab
   11. Isaac
   12. Lot
   13. Seth
   14. Ham
   15. Achan
   16. Melchizedek
   17. Manoah

5. **RELATIONSHIP BETWEEN ...?**
   1. brother and sister
   2. brothers
   3. father and son
   4. uncle and nephew
   5. cousins
   6. grandson and grandmother
   7. priest and helper
   8. sisters
   9. husband and wife

10. daughter-in-law and mother-in-law
11. close friends
12. uncle and nephew
13. husband and wife
14. brothers
15. mother and son
16. brothers
17. grandfather and grandson

6. MOTHERS IN THE BIBLE
1. Jochebed
2. Hannah
3. Ruth
4. Elisabeth
5. Eunice
6. Eve
7. Sarah
8. Hagar
9. Rebekah
10. Rachel
11. Leah
12. Bathsheba
13. Asenath
14. Naomi
15. Mary

7. BIBLE DETECTIVE
1. Paul
2. Samson
3. Moses
4. Zacchaeus
5. Jeremiah
6. Luke
7. Judas
8. John
9. Esau
10. John the Baptist
11. Belshazzar
12. Noah
13. Stephen
14. Jonah
15. Joseph
16. Rahab
17. Ruth
18. Samuel

8. WHO AM I?
1. Nathanael
2. Pilate
3. Rachel
4. Rebekah
5. Reuben
6. Samson
7. Solomon
8. Silas
9. Thomas
10. Mary, the Mother of Jesus
11. John Mark
12. Lot
13. Joseph
14. Luke
15. Abram
16. Gideon

9. HOW MANY?
1. forty
2. one
3. 350
4. six
5. two
6. 1,000
7. 150
8. four
9. as many as the dust of the earth; as many as the stars in the sky
10. eight
11. one
12. four
13. ten
14. one (Dinah)
15. six
16. six
17. three

10. TO WHOM DID GOD SAY . . . ?
1. Adam
2. Cain
3. Noah
4. Abraham
5. Jacob
6. Moses

7. Joshua
8. Gideon
9. Samuel
10. Solomon
11. Satan
12. David

11. WHO AM I?
1. Achan
2. Laban
3. Malachi
4. Methuselah
5. Naomi
6. Paul
7. Peter
8. Rachel
9. Rahab
10. Reuben
11. Samuel
12. Saul
13. Thomas
14. Timothy
15. Stephen
16. Onesimus
17. Abel

12. WHAT'S THE MISSING WORD?
1. "keeper"
2. "liveth"
3. "evil"
4. "wrath"
5. "faith"
6. "woman"
7. "comforted"
8. "heart"
9. "world"
10. "serve"
11. "given"
12. "charity"
13. "Word"
14. "knock"
15. "salt"
16. "snow"

13. FINISH THE PHRASE!
1. "risen"

2. "OF THE JEWS"
3. "wise"
4. "life"
5. "ashamed"
6. "reasonable service"
7. "thrice" (or three times)
8. "clay"
9. "rivers of water"
10. "die"
11. "thee"
12. "my people"
13. "his holy name"
14. "gospel of Christ"
15. "mocked"
16. "is right"

14. WHO AM I?
1. Aaron
2. Hur
3. Balaam
4. Benjamin
5. Daniel
6. Eli
7. Esther
8. Gideon
9. Herod
10. Hezekiah
11. Isaac
12. Jacob
13. Jeremiah
14. Jesse
15. Job
16. Jonathan

15. PRAYERS IN THE BIBLE
1. Abraham
2. Eliezer
3. Gideon
4. Hannah
5. David
6. Daniel
7. Jesus
8. Peter
9. Zacharias
10. the rich man
11. ten
12. Matthias

43

13. Stephen
14. Paul
15. Revelation

16. FACTS IN GENESIS
1. heaven
2. earth
3. sixth
4. "Let there be light."
5. the serpent
6. seventh
7. the tree of the knowledge of good and evil
8. fig leaves
9. animal skins
10. because the people were wicked
11. gopher wood
12. one
13. 600 years old
14. Shem, Ham, and Japheth
15. eight
16. a raven and a dove

17. PEOPLE IN GENESIS
1. Adam
2. Enoch
3. Ham
4. Abram and Jacob
5. Sarai
6. Lot
7. Hagar
8. Abraham
9. Keturah
10. Isaac
11. Esau
12. Jacob
13. Laban
14. Rachel
15. Joseph
16. Simeon

18. FACTS IN EXODUS
1. three days
2. straw
3. a serpent
4. It turned to blood.

5. frogs
6. darkness
7. all the firstborn
8. blood of a lamb
9. midnight
10. unleavened bread
11. They drowned in the Red Sea.
12. a tree
13. "manna"
14. A pillar of cloud by day, and a pillar of fire by night.
15. forty years

19. PEOPLE AND PLACES IN EXODUS
1. pharaoh
2. Moses
3. Jethro
4. Aaron
5. Miriam
6. Red Sea
7. Marah
8. Aaron and Hur
9. Sinai
10. Pharaoh's daughter
11. Zipporah
12. Levi
13. the magicians of Egypt
14. Joseph
15. Goshen

20. WHO SAID IT?
1. Adam
2. Cain
3. Abram
4. Lot
5. Isaac
6. Rebekah
7. Jacob
8. Esau
9. Joseph
10. the Egyptian baker
11. Miriam
12. Pharaoh's daughter
13. Moses
14. Pharaoh
15. Aaron

21. **MEN AND WOMEN OF ISRAEL**
1. Nun
2. Rahab
3. Achan
4. Caleb
5. Othniel
6. Eglon
7. Deborah
8. Gideon
9. Jephthah
10. Samson
11. Delilah

22. **MAN AFTER GOD'S OWN HEART**
1. Jesse
2. Saul
3. Jonathan
4. Goliath
5. five
6. Psalms
7. Philistines
8. harp
9. Samuel
10. Bathsheba
11. Uriah
12. Nathan
13. Absalom
14. Solomon
15. Jesus Christ

23. **ELIJAH AND ELISHA**
1. a raven
2. meal and oil never failed
3. Ahab
4. 450
5. Carmel
6. talking; or sleeping; or on a journey
7. Jezebel
8. by a whirlwind and with a chariot and horses of fire
9. mantle
10. Naaman
11. seven
12. Jordan
13. Gehazi
14. Two bears attacked them.
15. He made it float.

24. **DANIEL AND JONAH**
1. the presidents and the princes
2. Darius
3. He prayed.
4. sad
5. an angel
6. Daniel's accusers and their families
7. Nineveh
8. Tarshish
9. Joppa
10. sleeping
11. cast him overboard
12. He prayed.
13. three days and three nights
14. He arose and went.
15. repented of their evil

25. **THE BOY JESUS**
1. Mary
2. Joseph
3. Emmanuel
4. Caesar Augustus
5. Bethlehem
6. "Fear not"
7. in a manger
8. Egypt
9. gold, frankincense, and myrrh
10. Nazareth
11. Jerusalem
12. the Feast of the Passover
13. twelve
14. one day (or a day's journey)
15. three
16. "Sitting in the midst of the doctors, both hearing them, and asking them questions."
17. "God and man"

26. **HIS PARABLES**
1. rock

2. sand
3. Birds devoured it.
4. the Word of God
5. Those who receive the word, and bring forth fruit.
6. pull down his barns and build bigger
7. in the wilderness
8. lit a candle; swept the house
9. feeding swine
10. Pharisee
11. He said he would go, but he didn't.
12. We should let it shine so that others can see it.
13. false
14. a wedding garment

27. THE MIRACLE-WORKER
1. They lowered him through a hole they made in the roof.
2. "Stretch forth thy hand."
3. He raised him from the dead.
4. "swine" (pigs)
5. the "border" (hem)
6. about twelve years old
7. They laughed at Him.
8. five loaves and two fishes
9. Samaritan
10. "Jesus, thou son of David, have mercy on me."
11. sleeping
12. He began walking on the water toward Jesus.
13. seven
14. fill them with water
15. "Rise, take up thy bed, and walk."
16. Siloam
17. four days

28. JESUS OUR LORD
1. chief priests and elders
2. Pontius Pilate
3. Judas

4. thirty
5. He hanged himself.
6. Barabbas
7. two
8. three
9. "My God, my God, why hast thou forsaken Me?"
10. Joseph of Arimathaea
11. first
12. an angel
13. the disciples
14. The disciples had come in the night and stole his body away.
15. Thomas
16. Simon Peter

29. WHO SAID IT?
1. Mary
2. Elisabeth
3. John the Baptist
4. Nicodemus
5. Simon Peter
6. Judas Iscariot
7. Pilate
8. the angel at the tomb
9. Peter
10. Bartimaeus
11. shepherds
12. the good Samaritan
13. the publican
14. Zacchaeus
15. Jesus

30. FACTS ABOUT THE CHURCH
1. John and Romans
2. after
3. Jerusalem
4. Matthias
5. They spoke in other tongues.
6. Jesus would come again.
7. 3,000
8. They healed him.
9. They died immediately.
10. He was stoned.

11. Saul (Paul)
12. Philip
13. Isaiah

31. FACTS ABOUT PAUL
 1. Damascus; to imprison Christians.
 2. three days
 3. Tabitha (Dorcas)
 4. "Not so, Lord."
 5. Antioch
 6. "Thou art mad."
 7. Saul (Paul) and Barnabas
 8. midnight
 9. an earthquake
10. kill himself
11. "Sirs, what must I do to be saved?"
12. "Believe on the Lord Jesus Christ, and thou shalt be saved, and thy house."
13. Athens
14. Diana
15. Agrippa
16. He was bitten by a snake.

32. WHO SAID IT?
 1. Jesus
 2. Peter
 3. Gamaliel
 4. Stephen
 5. Philip
 6. the Ethiopian eunuch
 7. Saul (Paul)
 8. the Philippian jailor
 9. Gallio
10. Demetrius
11. Felix
12. Festus
13. Agrippa

Listen every week to the

CHILDREN'S BIBLE HOUR

Heard on a network of hundreds of stations around the world. For a complete list of radio outlets, write to Children's Bible Hour, Box 1, Grand Rapids, Michigan, 49501.